MILDRED NEWMAN and BERNARD BERKOWITZ are married to each other. They are psychoanalysts and psychologists, and practice in New York City.

"*How to Be Awake and Alive* is a new classic, even deeper, more personal, more vibrant than *How to Be Your Own Best Friend.*"
—Joseph Katz, Ph.D.

"*How to Be Awake and Alive* will enlighten anyone who reads it. Mildred Newman and Bernard Berkowitz lead us skillfully to the discovery of secret childhood patterns within ourselves. A truly readable, understandable work."
—Ruth Pirkle Berkeley, M.D.

"This book is not a simple recipe, formula or panacea 'how-to', but rather a 'how to' *understand.* Here are meaningful glimpses of the treatment process. Such lucid and poignant examples and illustrations are clarifying and useful. I recommend this book with enthusiasm."
—Saul Tuttman, M.D., Ph.D.

"*How to Be Awake and Alive* succeeds in bringing obscure psychoanalytic concepts within everyone's grasp. To be awake and alive is to be in tune and in touch."
—Iris A. Sangiuliano, Ph.D.

By the authors of
How to Be Your Own Best Friend

How to Be
Awake
and
Alive

Mildred
Newman
&
Bernard
Berkowitz

Random House New York

How to Be Awake and Alive

Library of Congress Cataloging in Publication Data:

Newman, Mildred, 1920–
How to be awake and alive.

1. Success.   I. Berkowitz, Bernard, 1918–   joint author.
II. Title.
BF637.S8N455   158'.1   74-29614
ISBN 0-394-49252-8

MANUFACTURED IN THE UNITED STATES OF AMERICA

24689753

First Edition

For Dr. Theodor Reik
and
The National Psychological Association
for Psychoanalysis

"In How to Be Your Own Best Friend, *Mildred Newman and Bernard Berkowitz distilled the wisdom of their years of psychoanalytic practice. Now, in this book, they share with us the specific dramatic moments which are the source of that wisdom. They capture the moments of change, the lightning flashes of illumination when the person awakens to the hidden meaning of his life's patterns. Don't go sleepwalking through the days of your life. Let these friends help you also to be awake and alive, as they helped the people you will meet in this book.*"

— Elizabeth Thorne, Ph.D.

How To Be Awake & Alive

Mildred Newman & Bernard Berkowitz

Millions of people are reading *How to Be Your Own Best Friend* and discovering a new and satisfying way to feel about themselves. Now, in their new book, *How to Be Awake and Alive*, Mildred Newman and Bernard Berkowitz again use their psychoanalytic wisdom to show in a common-sense way how those ideas, prejudices and fears that developed when we were very young can prevent us from achieving happiness today. They offer many intriguing illustrations from their extensive practice to guide the reader to a life that is Awake and Alive.

We have learned from each person who has come to us for help and whose life story we have used to help others.

We also gratefully acknowledge the many wise people of the past who have had the vision to see and describe by whatever name the life dreams of human beings.

1/
Sometimes people live their lives as if to protect the past

"I really love her. I always have such loving feelings for her, but whenever we're together, something happens. I get short-tempered, I pick on her for the smallest things, and then I feel rotten."

The young man in my* office was talking about his unhappy marriage. He loved his wife, but felt compelled to criticize her and put her down. As the session continued, he was asked about his parents. He shook his head sadly, saying he was sure they didn't love each other. He was encouraged to talk about his childhood, and it became increasingly clear that somehow it was important for him to believe that his parents had an unhappy marriage. Not only that, but he had an equally strong conviction that all marriages were bad, including his own.

To hold on to his belief about his parents' marriage, he had to see every marriage in the same way. (This was his way of making the present serve the past.)

* We are writing of our analytic experiences. "I" or "my" refers to either of us.

You mean some people actually want to control the past?

Yes. A person can live his life to protect a fantasy about the past. It almost seems as though he believes that what he does now can affect something *then*. We have seen many examples. This young man, as a child, felt that he was the favorite—that his mother really loved him best. But then he had to reconcile that feeling with the fact that his mother was living with "him"—that ogre, that brute—his father. He had to explain to himself why she was devoted to "him," why she served "him." He had to cope with the bad feeling he got when "they" went into the bedroom, closed the door and left him out there, all alone. In order to comfort himself and hold on to the feeling of being the favorite, he made up a little story that went something like this: "It's not that she loves him best, but she has to stay with him, because she is afraid and because she needs him to bring home money."

Marriage was, from this child's point of view, a matter of convenience and necessity. Certainly his belief was that people who are married don't love each other, and he devoted his adult life to proving it. Otherwise he risked having that "all alone and left out" feeling.

Isn't that a rather unusual story?

We have heard the same story from others, who say, "I look around and I don't see any good marriages. I don't see any loving couples. People have to stay together because they get lonely, they need to have someone support them, they need someone to do the cooking and the housework. There is no love in marriage." If these people who speak this way were to discover they loved their mates, it would shatter the myth of their childhood.

You know, that sounds like so many people who are vehemently against marriage. Do you mean that people who talk that way are just trying to prove their parents didn't love each other?

For some who take that position it could be the unconscious motivation. What we are really trying to say is that some people, many people, subject themselves to unhappiness for an idea which they no longer clearly remember but which was once important in childhood.

But so important that it continues to affect their lives for years and years? That's like letting a child run your life.

Exactly. It is just like letting the child in you run your life.

Isn't it ironic that an adult can be willing to give up the love in his own marriage in order to hold on to the belief that his parents didn't really love each other?

Yes, what a price to pay to hold on to the feeling of having been loved best. We have known people who have gone even further—people who have never allowed themselves to marry, or to have someone who loves them and whom they can love. Sometimes they say they'd like to get married, but they insist there just isn't anyone around who is suitable. *It is True*.

That's too bad.

There's a lovely young woman who didn't marry. Her father left her and her mother when she was five years old. She cried and cried and cried, and promised herself that never again in her whole life would anyone mean so much to her that she would ever again have to feel so bad. From that point on, until we saw her, she devoted her life to not having feelings for anyone. She would never let anyone mean anything to her. She saw one of us in private sessions, and we discovered that each time she got to the point where she had feelings for her analyst, she would find an excuse to leave treatment and not come back until she had wiped out those feelings. She did the same thing unconsciously whenever she became interested in a young man. She would find a reason to break off.

You said she did it unconsciously. What do you mean by that?

What is unconscious is a secret from yourself. It may be evident to others, but as the saying goes, you are often the last to know. It is what you have thought and felt, and forgotten and hidden. We mean not only a single idea or feeling but, rather, whole systems of thinking, entire ways of looking at the world and yourself—ways which influence your life, and though outside of your awareness, are inside of you. These ways of thinking and feeling have been described as life styles, life scripts, scenarios, life commands and blueprints. Many wise people have pointed out that we don't always do what we think we are doing, but even though this truth has been repeated many times, it is still a bit difficult to understand and describe.

Many people move through life as though acting out private dreams, and we would like to describe their dreams in the hope that you may find some clues to your own. We have helped some of these dreamers to awaken from a life dream. Perhaps we can make it possible for you to share their experience.

6

2/
If you ask a fish about his world, the last thing he can describe is water

How do I know any of what you're saying about life dreams applies to me? I know I get up every morning and go about my day. I don't feel I'm not awake. How can I tell if I'm one of the people living a dream and not knowing it?

The people who came to us, the people whose experiences we are describing here, did not know that they were living out a childhood fantasy either. It is only after awakening, and coming out of it, that they were able to look back and see that the tight fist of a determined child had been ruling their lives.

But what about me? To come out of it, wouldn't I first have to know I'm in a dream?

Yes, knowing you're in a dream—that's the difficulty. If you ask a fish about his world, the saying goes, the last thing he can describe is water. We live in our own self-created forest, and all we can see are the trees. Only the sick can appreciate good health, an Arab proverb says. We exist in our own emotional atmosphere, which we have created and which, of course, we take for granted. It is truly a problem of having to transcend oneself!

Enough. You've convinced me it's not easy—but can't you give me some hints?

Fair enough. If you can review your own life, and see a tendency for your experiences to fall into a pattern of mishaps, then you can be pretty sure you are living a dream. Because a dream is a self-fulfilling prophecy. If things always "happen" to you, if people always mistreat you in a certain way, if you discover you frequently feel misunderstood—then there's a possibility you have something that needs investigating. You may be looking at life through your own specially tinted glasses.

Any other hints? What if I can't see any of those patterns in my life?

Well, how do you feel about other people? Do you have a consistent bias about what some people are like? Do you always get annoyed with: older men, younger men, older women, younger women, bald men, short men, tall men? If you can readily see that your feelings about certain kinds of people are in some sort of rut, then you may very well know you're living a dream and you could be close to figuring out what your life dream is all about.

I see. Any other hints?

✳ Are you the kind of person who says, "I never have enough time for anything or anyone," even though you may not be accomplishing very much with your time? It could be that you are too involved in your fantasies. Are you distracted easily? Forgetful? Do your friends complain that often you are not really listening? Do you sometimes discover that you haven't quite understood what was being said or that you're not aware of what was going on around you?

Well, that gives me something to think about.

It's good to think about yourself. Perhaps it will help you understand if we tell you about more people living in dreams.

A man came to see us, and it was clear from listening to him that he was living his life to prove something to his father. It was as if his father were walking at his side, criticizing him, and he was living his life arguing with his "bad" father. At first he had no conscious sense of what he was doing. But after a while he became aware that his life was one long struggle to justify himself to his disapproving father . . . who had been dead for many years.

I think I'm beginning to understand what you mean about conscious and unconscious.

What is unconscious is a secret from yourself.

But could you give more examples?

Yes, we can.

A young patient, a talented psychiatric social worker, never believed in the unconscious, though he had studied a great deal of psychology and psychoanalysis.

"I need proof," he would say. At one point in his analysis, we came to a time when we were discussing homosexuality. This was for him a frightening topic, and he left the session appearing upset.

He returned the next day, lay down on the couch and said, "I can't think of anything to say, I have nothing to tell you."

I said, "Maybe that relates to what we were talking about yesterday."

"I don't know what we were talking about yesterday. Are you going to tell me what we were talking about yesterday?"

I said, "No."

He said, "I have nothing to say, nothing to say."

Then I said, "Well, why don't you pick something on my desk, and just talk about it?"

I had on my desk a vase with a single rose in it.

He said angrily, "What do you want me to do? Talk about that sweet william on your desk?"

It was a particularly strange question because he was a person who prided himself on knowing the name of every tree and every flower, so when I said, "What did you say?" he started to laugh and said, "Oh, I said sweet william, and it's a rose, of course."

And I said, "Right."

And then he said, "Now I remember. We were talking about homosexuality yesterday!"

And that was proof. After that he truly believed in the unconscious.

The unconscious is a difficult concept to understand, and as you have just seen, even people in psychology, social work and psychiatry, or studying to be therapists or analysts, sometimes resist the concept of the unconscious.

A young psychology student was referred to me. I asked her why me, and she said, "I am looking for a woman analyst who does not believe in the penis-envy theory." (Freud's penis-envy theory holds that women feel inferior to men because of the anatomical difference.)

I looked at her and said, "You just convinced me."

My response angered her, but nevertheless she decided to come into treatment with me. She would often talk about how she believed in the unconscious, ". . . but it's a theoretical belief." Of course "everybody has an unconscious," but she was not convinced that she did.

One day she walked in laughing. When she had stopped, she said, "I had a remarkable experience last night. I was watching a TV program, and there were some women dancers wearing very tight leotards. I realized suddenly that I was looking at each one to see if I could see her penis, and then I finally understood what you meant when I first came here and told you I was looking for a woman analyst who doesn't believe in the penis-envy theory and you said, "You just convinced me!"

I guess she started out by protesting too much that first day. Could that be a clue?

Yes. And here's another clue. Think of a favorite joke or story. Is there one you like to tell again and again? When you do that, it is almost as if you have unfinished business with the theme you keep coming back to.

Let us tell you some favorite stories of people we've known and what they have meant to the tellers.

3/
Kreplach!

Here is a striking example of how people can unknowingly telegraph the truth about themselves by telling and retelling a favorite story. A beautiful young woman repeatedly told me the "kreplach story." (Kreplach are little three-cornered meat-filled crepes, like won ton or ravioli.)

She would start by saying, "Did you ever hear the joke about kreplach?"

I would say, "Tell it to me."

And she would.

"There was a young boy who had a kreplach phobia. Every time he would see kreplach, he would scream. His screams were so upsetting to his mother that she took him to a therapist, who said, 'Oh, this is a very simple problem. Take him home and make kreplach from beginning to end and let him follow each step, and then he won't scream any more.'

"So the mother did just that. She started with the flour, and said, 'Are you afraid of this?' And the little boy said, 'No!'

"Then she rolled the flour and showed him the dough, and said, 'Are you afraid of this?' And again he said, 'No!'

"Then she showed him the chopped meat and said, 'Do you know what this is?' He said, 'Yes!' And she said, 'Are you frightened of this?' He said, 'No!'

"Then she put the meat in the dough, and still he wasn't frightened, but when she made the corners and put it altogether, he shrieked, 'Kreplach!' and was very frightened."

I wondered why the young woman kept telling me this story. Then it came to me that in a sense this was the story of her life. She was a young woman who would meet a man who was unsuccessful, build him up, and when he was a "man" she would scream "Kreplach!" and become very frightened of him.

First there was the unsuccessful playwright whom she encouraged to write a Broadway hit, and then there was a man who was suicidal and one who was a drug addict. She helped each of them to become healthy and strong and successful. But as soon as a man was functioning and could stand on his own two feet and didn't need her to "carry" him, she would, in effect, scream "Kreplach!" and find a way to drop him and go on to the next unsuccessful man.

It was not until I could make the connection between the story and her life, and she could understand that connection, that she could face her problem: she could not stand being with a man who was independent and self-sufficient.

As long as the man was dependent, she could feel grown

up. As soon as the man could take care of himself, she began to feel uncomfortably "little."

That's startling—to tell a simple joke and reveal so much about herself. Do you have another example of how a person's favorite story provided an important clue to his life dream?

Well, there was another engaging young woman who told me the story of Graham Greene's *The Potting Shed*, but it was her personal version of the play. As she told it, it was about a priest whose young nephew of fourteen, who was visiting him, was struck by lightning in the potting shed. The priest prayed to God and promised Him that he, the priest, would give up the thing he loved most if the nephew was saved. The nephew was spared, and the priest gave up God.

After the patient had told me this story twice, I began to connect it with the story of her life—bits and pieces of which she had been telling me over a period of a year or so. This young woman could remember when she was five years old, watching her mother work around the house and thinking that if her mother would go away, she could be the mother in the house, not the child. She could take care of her daddy and no longer feel small and left out. How wonderful it would all be.

When she was about seven, her mother went to the hospital to have an operation, and died. Secretly and fearfully, the child believed it was her wish that killed her mother, that she had the power of life and death. And from that moment on, she who had loved her father so much could not bear his presence. She would spend her days thinking about him and how wonderful it would be when he came home from work. When he did, she would hate him and not have anything to do with him. Having gotten her wish for her mother to go away, she had to give up what she loved the most—her father.

Continuing her life dream in her marriage, she adored her husband as long as he was away; all day she would wait longingly for him. He abetted her by ignoring her when he came home from work every night. They would hardly exchange a word all evening; together they had unconsciously worked out a very ingenious arrangement.

The husband came into therapy, understood what he was doing, and stopped avoiding his wife. That broke their bargain.

Then she had to leave the house at night to avoid him. Until she understood her problem, she could not be with him. As in *The Potting Shed*, she had to give up the person she loved best.

You mean, through her version of The Potting Shed, *this woman was really telling you that she had the power of life and death?*

Exactly, though she was not conscious of it, she believed herself the possessor of awesome powers. But it is not unusual for some children to resent their small and helpless state, and imagine themselves all-powerful. In such a child's mind, wishing someone dead can feel the same as being a murderer.

But the thought is not the deed.

We will never forget the ten-year-old girl who was brought to us suffering from what is called "school phobia." The child could not attend school. She would go every morning, but when she got there she became violently ill and would have to be sent home. She was never sick when she was at home. Finally the school authorities suggested to her family that she be kept out for a while. After she had not attended school for about six months, her parents sent her into treatment.

After a number of sessions we were able to piece together the following:

She had gone on a trip to the West with her father to attend a family function. Her mother stayed home. Sleeping arrangements were such that she and her father shared a bed, sleeping head to toe, and when she awakened the first morning, she was very frightened and insisted that they leave immediately. Nothing could calm her, and she was taken home. In therapy, she discovered that when she had awakened and found herself alone with her father, she felt something terrible must have happened, and she believed it was that her mother was dead. She had to go home to see for herself that her mother was all right. And she had to keep staying home from school to protect her mother, to, so to speak, keep her alive. She was finally able to understand that the person she was protecting her mother from was herself.

Another child who had her wish come true. But do you mean every time a kid points a finger and goes "bang-bang," he really thinks he's killing someone?

Not at all. If a child can openly say, "Bang—you're dead," that's healthy. It's the child whose death wish is a guilty secret who is more likely to be in trouble.

There is another example of the way in which a person's favorite story can be a tip-off to his inner life. A man who was in treatment with one of us was a brilliant administrator, but somehow could never rise to the number-one spot no matter where he worked. On a number of occasions he referred to "The Bear," a William Faulkner story which had moved him deeply.

As the patient told the story, there was a rural village which was subjected to the raids of a large and wily bear; it would come down out of the mountains and carry off livestock and do other damage. Each year a posse of farmers would try in vain to hunt him down. One time a young man was out hunting alone. Suddenly he had the legendary great bear in his rifle sights, but he could not pull the trigger. As he lowered the gun he thought of his father and all the men of the town who had been unable to bring down this quarry. He could not allow himself to be better than they!

In his analysis, the patient was asked to think about what possible meaning this favorite story could have in his life. When he saw the connection, he began to deal with his inability to be number one.

That's helpful. Do you have any more shortcuts to tuning in on your own life dreams?

Yes. What is your earliest memory? When you have that, go on and ask yourself, "What is the earliest memory of mother, of father?"—if they are not included in your first memory. Alfred Adler was the psychiatrist who first showed how these very early memories could provide important clues to the way you looked at life as a child.

A young woman was thrown into a state of panic when her boyfriend proposed to her. She had been going with him for a while, and liked him, but when he asked her to marry him she had a severe anxiety attack, so severe it sent her into analysis. As she talked about her life, she admitted she had worked hard to get this young man to love her. But when she succeeded, she wanted to run away from him.

I asked for her first memory of her father. This is what she remembered. One day when she was a little girl—probably four or five—she had a fight with her mother. She told her father how angry she was with her mother, and he said, "Go upstairs and pack your little suitcase, and I'll take you away with me."

She was very happy, and went upstairs and packed her suitcase. When she came down they got in the car. He drove around the block a few times, and then took her to visit some friends who lived just around the corner. When she saw where they were, she realized he had been teasing her, only joking, and her joy faded. She was furious with him and never forgave him.

This experience became her dream, the fantasy of betrayal she relived again and again. When she found a young man who really wanted her, she had to let him down. He had broken her dream. He had betrayed her by not betraying her.

Here is the first memory, from about age three, of a man who was not as successful as his talents warranted:

"We were vacationing at the beach. I went into a store and sang, and people gave me money. As I started for our cottage I saw my father approach, and quickly dropped the coins through the cracks in the boardwalk. He had warned me never to take money from strangers."

I see that connection all right, but something else is puzzling me. We keep talking about life dreams, but what about the dreams we have at night? Is there a connection between the two kinds of dreams?

Of course there is a connection, especially if you pay attention to a dream which you have had more than once. That is really a sign you are trying to tell yourself something. After all, dreams are not caused by indigestion. They are messages to you from yourself. It has been said that a dream that is not understood is like a letter that hasn't been opened.

You can also find valuable clues in your daydreams and fantasies. Do you remember the character Walter Mitty, who was created by James Thurber? He was the fellow who would go off into grandiose daydreams in which he was always the hero conquering the bad guys. While lost in his daydream, Mitty was letting life pile up around him. His wish to be top man can be a healthy one and is shared by many people. However, it also can contain a trap: that kind of success is sometimes achieved only at the expense of killing or hurting other people.

We know a man who came into analysis and impressed us with his mild, appealing manner. After a while he jokingly confessed that he was still pointing his finger at people and "killing" them. Another man had an elaborate going-to-sleep fantasy. He would start out as a convicted murderer on death row. The President of the United States would arrange to have him secretly released from prison to carry out some daring and dangerous act of assassination for the purpose of "national security."

Other people, as they go about their lives, are haunted by the feeling of being hunted, pursued and in danger of being caught and punished without reason. All of these feelings can be clues to your own life dream and keys to understanding yourself.

I'm glad to learn I'm not so different. I have some of those same fantasies and daydreams. I'm learning there is a great deal going on inside of me that I'm often not aware of.

That's not surprising. Everyone has an inner world, and it is endlessly fascinating to explore.

Won't I become too introspective, too wrapped up in myself and out of touch with the real world?

Perhaps for a little while. But a life that's examined is more worth living. In the long run you will see the real world more clearly if you are not looking at it through your own private distortions.

4/
Someday...!

"Someday . . . you'll see!" The solemn pledge of the hurt child echoes through the years.

At one time each of us has been the smallest; each of us has felt helpless; and some of us have had to comfort ourselves with "I'll show them . . . someday."

It is painful for a child to discover that the world does not revolve around him, especially if he has been helped by indulgent parents to believe that he is the center of the family. It hurts to be laughed at, punished, mocked, excluded by other children and by adults. It can hurt, too, when the new baby comes. The child feels a little better when he can wrap himself in fantasies of "Someday . . . I'll get even."

This vow can become the spark for burning ambition, for dedicated and determined hard work. The voyage from feeling like a "nobody" to feeling like a "somebody" can be a very satisfying part of growing up. But sometimes these feelings can be distorted. People can get into difficulty with themselves and the world when their ambition is mainly to get even, to return hurt for hurt, to destroy. What can you expect when the child in you runs your life? The child feels hurt, but doesn't dare hurt back. The child broods, and through brooding, creates a comforting scenario. All those people who push him around may not know it, he muses, but he is working on a plan to be the most powerful, dangerous, scary person on earth. (You may be sure that "he" could just as easily read "she.")

Someday, when he grows up, he'll show them—bullets, knives, atomic and hydrogen bombs, death rays . . . or becoming the most fatally seductive person in the world. There is no limit to vengeful ingenuity. Hurt little John has a secret which helps him to feel strong, to have patience to endure the lowly status of childhood. He is just waiting for the day. Meanwhile he must hold on to the anger, feed it, polish it, nurse the grudge, and collect new injustices, because the anger makes him feel strong, the anger helps him feel superior—it is the secret weapon against feelings of insignificance and nothingness. Anger thus becomes the guiding star for life's voyage. Anger becomes the foundation, the cornerstone of the whole person. Anger becomes the altar upon which all of life is sacrificed.

That sounds grim but true. I do know people who seem to be angry at everyone and everything all the time.

Not just the openly angry ones, but there are the "nice" ones who hide their anger from themselves and others. They regard themselves as kindly and well-intentioned. As they see it, their troubles are always caused by the hostility of others.

Let us tell you about such a man—we'll call him Chuck—a tall rangy Westerner with an infectious smile and many talents. While working his way through college, he started an ingenious business, which was still flourishing when he left school. He didn't finish college, although his grades were good. Non-finishing was his trademark.

Chuck went to acting school, got some off-Broadway parts and was marked as a "comer." Then came his big chance. He auditioned brilliantly and was offered a leading part, which he accepted. This happened three times and each time the story was the same. Before the contracts could be signed, he somehow managed to feel exploited and put-upon. He would get into an argument with the producer or the director over some insignificant detail, and then he was through.

Even his analysis was like that—a brilliant start which fizzled. He didn't stay long, and left treatment pretty much unchanged. He did learn one thing about himself, though—his need for vengeance. He had grown up in a home that had been a continuous battlefield. He thought he had gotten over his anger at his bickering parents. One day in a therapy session he was asked to close his eyes and imagine his name in lights—the star of the theater on Main Street in his hometown. Then he was asked to imagine his parents walking by, proudly pointing to their son's name and his picture in front of the theater. His face flushed, he pounded his fists, opened his eyes, stood up and shouted, "No, no, they don't deserve it—never!" He would rather be a failure, a nobody, than give them that kind of pleasure, that kind of satisfaction. He was living his life *against* his parents, which put them in the center of his existence, just as surely as if he were living his life *for* them. He wouldn't give his analyst the pleasure of helping him, either.

That reminds me of that British movie The Loneliness of the Long Distance Runner. *Do you remember that from several years ago? It was about a young man in reform school who ran his heart out until he felt betrayed by the headmaster, whom he had considered his friend. Toward the end of the big race, he is about to win, he is just a few hundred yards from the finish—he stops, folds his arms and just stands there as the others catch up and pass him. You could see the hate in his eyes.*

Yes, that has the same trademark: "Show great promise, but don't finish—that will break their hearts." Incidentally, playwrights, novelists and poets have long known about these feelings.

It is incredible how likable some spiteful people are, and how hard they work at perfecting their skills. The build-up, before the letdown, is impressive. We recall a very charming fellow who could sell almost anyone anything anytime. We had to keep him from spellbinding his therapy group with his magnificent command of language. It was easy to see how he could make several small fortunes. It was painful to all who knew him to see him blow it each time in high-stakes poker sessions. He was not a compulsive gambler in the usual sense. He only got the itch when he was in danger of becoming the comfortable middle-class success his family expected him to be. He did the same sort of thing with the women in his life—building up hopes and expectations, and then cruelly letting them down—not quickly, but torturously by slow degrees.

The pattern of his life was easy to see by the time he was in his mid-thirties, but like Chuck's, not easy to give up. He would say, "Give up my anger? Never! My anger is my weapon; without it I feel defenseless and vulnerable."

I'm getting the hang of this. Don't you think it's possible that he was not only frustrating his parents but avoiding being as big a man as his father?

You are quite right. The spiteful person won't give his parents the pleasure of his success. Both of these men were not too proud to borrow money from home. It served to emphasize their failure and dependency.

I see. By the way, does this happen only to men?

No. Not at all. We were just going to tell you about the young woman her group called "The Little Match Girl."

She came into our office looking very pathetic. She wore a torn sweater and was unwashed and unkempt. The friend who brought her explained that she lived in a roach-infested, garbage-strewn, unlit apartment that she never left. She would often go without eating. But there was a mischievous glint in her eye that shone through the tangle of hair that fell over her face. I caught that look and she saw that I caught it.

The previous year she had graduated with honors from a respected New England college, and had started what looked like a promising career in advertising. She was intelligent, beautiful, and had many suitors. The abrupt change in her life seemed to take place about the time one of these young men wanted to marry her. After that, she made herself unattractive in order to discourage dates.

We had been working together for some months, and she was beginning to take better care of herself, when we got talking about marriage. I said, "Use your imagination and tell me—how would it feel to be married?" She thought a few moments and then burst out angrily, "Goddammit, I don't care if I never get married, because that's going to make *them* too happy, and they won't have to think or worry about me any more!" It was clear that her anger had surfaced to change her behavior at a point in her development when she might have moved away from her parents' protection.

She came into analysis because her wealthy parents were being too complacent about her rotting away. They just didn't seem to care enough. Also, she wanted them to pay for her therapy, since money meant a great deal to them. She was living her life not only out of revenge, but out of the need to stay connected to her parents.

I guess being connected is important.

Yes, and there are many different ways of being connected.

A young woman, who had been another analyst's patient for some years, came to see me. At the beginning of one of our early sessions I noticed that in the first five minutes she had quickly smoked three cigarettes.

I said, "Would you mind not smoking for a little while? It would be helpful for us to understand why you're smoking so much."

She replied, "I will not stop smoking. This is my session. I'm paying for it and I'll smoke when I damn well want to, and besides, I don't like the way you asked me not to smoke."

I was not going to be sidetracked, and said, "Oh, I'm

sorry, perhaps I said it harshly, but I didn't mean to. I just want to understand what's going on."

She refused to stop smoking during that session, but during the next four or five, she didn't touch a cigarette. I did not mention the fact that she was not smoking, nor did I question her about it. At each session, though, she commented on the fact that her throat hurt. At the sixth session, she asked if I knew anything about cancer of the throat. I told her that I was, as she knew, a psychologist, not a physician, and she should, of course, have her throat looked at by a medical doctor. But wasn't it remarkable that she had not been able to stop smoking when I asked her to, just for a little while, and now wasn't it strange that she hadn't been able to stop listening to me for two weeks? I said, "I didn't want you to listen to me forever—I just wanted you to stop smoking for a few minutes."

In the past she had always fought her mother. Indeed, the battling was so severe that she had been sent abroad to school at an early age.

I told her, "I truly understand why you cannot be your own person. You always disagreed with your mother, and now you're compelled to listen to her ceaselessly, though she is three thousand miles away."

The young woman was at first stunned, and then she sobbed and said through her tears, "It's not fair. You have discovered my secret. I'm so ashamed. I kept it for five years from my last analyst, and now it's out. I can't stop listening to my mother, all day long, every day. Now I understand how this has been affecting my life."

Now, let me see if I understand this. She couldn't do what you asked her to do, and had to have a sore throat instead.

Yes, the sore throat was her way of listening to me.

We are reminded of a woman who went off on a two-week vacation with her husband and children. When she came to her session after her vacation, I greeted her, and said, "Did you have a good vacation?"

She looked at me angrily, and said, "What—and give you pleasure?"

She was treating me as if I were her mother.

There was an interior decorator who was very negative in her attitude toward her husband. For example, he would ask her to please get solid-blue sheets and pillow-cases for their bed. But since she preferred patterned bed linens, she always bought them despite his preference. Finally his birthday came, and she told me in her session that she had been thinking of her inability to give him what he wanted, and for his birthday she had just bought him solid-color bed linens.

I was very moved, and said, "Oh, at last, how wonderful he'll have his blue sheets!"

She replied, "Blue? Of course not! I bought yellow sheets and cases. Don't you think yellow is a prettier color?"

She was treating her husband with the same sort of spiteful negativism that some people feel toward their parents. Just think of some typically adolescent situation. The teenager who comes home from school, throws his books on the table, his coat on the couch, thereby stirring into action his exasperated parent, who predictably screams, "How many times have I told you—when you come home, put your things away in their place?" These are the opening bars in a waltz which can go on for hours and in which both partners know all the steps.

The incidents that follow occurred after the people involved were well past their teens, but adolescent behavior is not restricted to adolescents.

A young man of twenty-four would never say hello or goodbye when he came to visit his parents. When they asked him why, he'd say, "I know you're sitting there waiting for me to say hello. That's why I can't do it."

A sweet young woman told me she thought about her father constantly, but resented his asking her to call home. Since she never called him, he would telephone once a month, and his calls felt like reproaches to her. To help resolve her conflict, I suggested that she call him whenever she thought about him; she would then not have to think about him all the time. At first she could not do this; she was as reluctant to take my suggestion as she had been to listen to her father. But when I said this might be a way of putting her father out of her mind, rather than allowing him to impose himself on her life, she found the idea appealing. She discovered that calling him once or twice a week helped to free her mind for other things.

Of course, there was much more involved than a phone call. It became clear to her how much of her energy she was devoting to fighting her father. With this understanding, she felt freer and more aware of her life in the present.

I never thought of that before. How much time I've wasted . . .

Don't reproach yourself. It's good that you can think about it now.

While a colleague was on vacation, I was seeing one of his patients, a writer who had never published any of his work. Indeed, he would write, but then he'd stuff his material away and never even show it to anyone. He lived alone in a one-room furnished flat. Most of the time he cooked his meals furtively on a hot plate, which he was forbidden to keep in his room. It was a special treat for him to eat in the local Automat or cafeteria. He supported himself by working at temporary jobs that paid minimum wages. He had been born in the South and his father had died when he was only four years old. His desperate mother put him in an orphanage far from home, so she could work. She visited him about once a year, each time promising that soon he could come home. He waited patiently at first. When he was sixteen years old she kept her promise. By this time it meant nothing to him any more, and he left home and came to New York.

I saw him only a few times, but with this understanding of his life dream, I said to him, "You know, I guess if you ever got a job, and had a decent place, and a telephone, and all the other things people have, it would be as if you were telling the world that you had a good mother—and you'll be damned if you want anybody to think that, after what she did to you."

He heard me, and this was the beginning of his being able to use the talents he did have.

Couldn't it also mean that in his fantasy he was still waiting for that great "someday" when his mother would make good that promise?

Yes, then he would still have had a good mother.

You might be interested in a different kind of "someday" story, about someone who seemed to be a great worldly success. A man in his mid-thirties was referred to us; he was keenly intelligent, aggressive and alert, and had achieved spectacular business success at an early age.

He said very sadly, "I've made millions of dollars and now I don't know what to do with my life. Everything is gray."

The man's plight could, of course, be explained by the fact that he had narrowed his interests and constricted his goals to making money; having done that, life seemed to hold no purpose for him, except to make more.

I asked him, "What was your idea of what would happen to you once you made your pile?"

He answered, "I often used to have the fantasy that someday I would be standing on top of a mountain, higher than everybody. Then I could look down on everyone, and say, 'The hell with you all. I don't need any of you. I don't have to be nice to you any more. I don't care if you all drop dead!'"

As he later realized, he was talking about his parents, and about his childhood life dream: he would become strong enough and secure enough so he would never need the love and protection of his parents. Then he would be able to get rid of them, get them out of his life, and be able to express all the anger and resentment of the years when he had been too frightened to tell them how he felt. After some time in treatment, when he could understand why there was no place to go when he reached the top, he became free of his depression.

He came in one day, saying, "Something has changed. I walk down the street now and I feel so alive. It's as though I had been sleepwalking all my life."

The awakening of this man is so impressive because he had seemed to be so successfully alive.

The personal pledge of vengeance—"Someday, when I grow up, I'll show them"—is like an IOU. It is like borrowing against the future. To achieve self-esteem in a dismal and unhappy present, the growing child borrows against fantasies of strength and retribution in the future.

The more horrible the fantasies of vengeance, the greater is the need to postpone the day of reckoning.

So the achievement of adulthood must be postponed. The time of such a life dream is always—"tomorrow." Life is not lived in the present, but is continually put off. To grow up means to fulfill that awful promise or to face the painful truth that it was all wishful thinking.

I guess it's a good idea to wake up from your dream before you get what you want.

Yes, "beware thy prayers, they may be answered."

Many years ago Dr. Theodor Reik told us a remarkable story of a New York woman who lived her life on the west side of Central Park, daydreaming and longing for a penthouse on Fifth Avenue across the park. Her wish was granted when her husband's business associate was forced to leave the country and presented her husband with his opulently furnished Fifth Avenue penthouse in lieu of the large amount of money he owed him.

The woman got her wish and moved into the penthouse, but instead of being happy, she became anxious and depressed. She worried about the safety and well-being of the people she loved. She was afraid that something dreadful might happen. After some years of analysis she discovered the cause of her fears. She believed that:

If her good wishes came true, her bad wishes might also come true.

Some people are afraid of success.

5/
I'm angry
unto death

Parents have a built-in response to a child's crying, or even to an expression of sadness or a sign of distress. Some children learn to play on this response by looking unhappy and sad. This blackmail can become, for a child, a powerful means of controlling adults.

That sounds awful. What can parents do to prevent it from happening?

If the parents feel confident that they have done right by their child, they will not allow themselves to be blackmailed. It is when they feel guilty that they run into problems. If they are reminded too much of themselves as children and forget they are the parents, then they are more apt to give in whenever their child's expression clouds over. In either case, the child is likely to decide that his sulking works. We see many people in our office who give the impression of angry children, pouting to have their way. One of the earliest and best descriptions of this kind of depression, carried to extremes, is in the Bible. Do you remember the story of Nineveh in the Book of Jonah?

As we recall it, God was troubled by the goings-on in Nineveh, and sent Jonah to warn the people to mend their ways or they would be destroyed. Jonah delivered God's message, but the people paid no attention. God, however, could not bring Himself to destroy His own creations, much to Jonah's disappointment. Jonah disappeared, and God found him sitting bareheaded in the desert under a blazing sun that could quickly fry him to a crisp. God asked him what was going on, and Jonah's answer is a psychiatric classic. He said, "Lord, I do well to be angry even unto death!" And God had mercy on His servant and caused a shade tree to grow over him and protect him.

I see we haven't changed so much since Biblical times. But is it so "sick" to have a moment of rage or disappointment when you have the feeling that life itself doesn't matter?

Of course not. Our concern is with people who elevate that moment to a way of life. There are people who are like the child who threatens to hold his breath and turn blue if not given his way. There is the person who learned how to drive his parents up the wall by putting on a long, sad face. Now he is doing the same thing, even though his parents are no longer there. What's more, he has come to believe in his own sadness. It may start out as an act, but—like "method" actors—to make it believable, the actor must become convinced of the reality of his feelings. So there is a deepening spiral of sadness, desolation, hopelessness, abandonment. The fog of depression always seems to thicken. The gloom gets deeper and deeper. It becomes unnerving and frightening, not only to the audience but to the "actor" himself.

I can recognize what you are saying about children, and I can even remember putting on little pleading expressions myself to get treats . . . but adults?

Sad. But true. Remember the "Little Match Girl" story we told you? She was going into a classic depression, with all the signs of deep melancholy. It's significant that she was not taking care of herself.

Is not taking care of oneself an important sign?

Quite often.

Very early in my practice, I was treating a woman who was very depressed. One day she came in and told me she was thinking of killing herself. As I listened to her, I found myself admiring her blouse and wondering who had ironed it so perfectly. I scolded myself for doing this—"How can you be so callous? This poor woman is talking about killing herself and you're wondering who ironed her blouse."

At that moment my patient said, "I did all my ironing yesterday."

The experience was very frightening to me. But as I thought about it that evening, I realized what had gone through my mind: "She is dressed perfectly. Her blouse is ironed exquisitely. How can she be getting ready to kill herself?"

The experience helped me to trust my own perceptions.

Okay. The woman with the pressed blouse wasn't really suicidal, and "The Little Match Girl" was putting on an act, and getting herself caught up in it. Then what is depression?

There have been volumes written on the subject. There is the kind which occurs in infants who have no mothering. After a while a neglected infant will stop crying. Even though all the physical needs, including food, are met, the emotionally neglected infant will go into a decline, and eventually die, just pine away. All these infants need is for someone to hold them, talk to them, sing, hum. In understaffed foundling wards, babies did die despite adequate physical care, until volunteers were brought in to give them a few hours of human contact each day. Did the uncared-for infants know they were unloved, unwanted? Maybe it's just a physical response to a physical presence. There have been some experiments with baby monkeys who were given cloth "mothers." They did better than the ones without any mothering, but they never grew up quite normally. *not feel it is ~~enough~~ true*

Among humans, some of the most depressed people look as though they feel completely deserted, with no one to care for them, no one to love them. We are not talking about the person who has just lost a loved one and is in mourning. He is experiencing grief which is to be expected. The bereaved person needs to feel loved. He needs to be reminded that there is human solace in the world. It is important to allow time for grieving, and gradually the mourning is less profound. But the person who is in a depression clings to the feeling, and will not take comfort from anyone. Even though there may be usually no direct expression of anger, there seems to be a stubborn insistence on unhappiness and sadness. Indeed, the sadness seems an essential ingredient of the personality. One person in a deep depression, when asked about her sadness, said, "I suffer, therefore I exist." Sometimes the suffering of the depression is like a constant companion, an antidote to loneliness, as well as an important part of identity.

It is still very difficult to understand why anyone would seek and cling to such sadness–that's crazy.

You know, "crazy" only means that we don't understand enough of what the person is getting out of it.

Sometimes the sadness serves as camouflage. Acting as if no one loved him felt like protection to one man. He grew up feeling his mother loved him best, and of course he loved her best. This was his guilty secret. Since his mother was unhappy in her marriage and showed it, the son had a ready model to follow. When he came into treatment he had completely "forgotten" how his depression got started. All he knew was that he felt depressed.

One day he came in complaining about how awful he felt. After a while I said to him, "You know, there must be something you get out of feeling so terrible. Maybe every time you tell me you feel awful, you are taking out that wonderful secret about you and your mother. Hidden away deep inside the sadness is the precious secret of you and your mother, loving each other."

He squirmed and said, "I don't know what you're talking about."

I said, "You remind me of a bad joke."

He eyed me balefully and with suspicion. "What do you mean?"

"I mean you and your mother. You remind me of the story of the farmer who heard a cackling and a commotion in the henhouse. He rushed up, cocking the hammers of his shotgun, and roared, 'Who's in there?' A high-pitched voice answered, 'Nobody in here but us chickens.'"

He glowered at me for a long minute and then he laughed. He laughed with relief. His secret was out. "You know, I always did have the feeling of my dad coming after me," he said as he laughed again.

That laughter is the analyst's reward. The patient is relieved and "tickled." He is suddenly free of the need to cover up.

Sometimes people hold on to their dreams through grief. Listen to this story a patient once told to her group. She had been having a love affair with a man and they had just separated.

"I was on my way here feeling very sad. I thought, I know what is going to happen, I'll get to that group and one of you will say, 'Well, what would you be feeling if you weren't feeling so sad,' and I thought, But I have to feel sad, because that is all I have left of him. If I let that go, there isn't anything more between us; then he is really gone."

Many dreams are like that. They are all that is left of someone, and holding on to that connection seems more important than fighting the sadness.

The best antidote to depression is anger, and that is not so strange when you consider that depression is most often anger turned against yourself. It is impossible to be in a depression and openly angry at the same time. At times this presents the analyst with the need to goad and provoke a patient who is already suffering deeply. Sometimes you have to hurt in order to help.

A long time ago I was seeing a twenty-six-year-old woman. She had had episodes of deep suicidal depression from the time she was sixteen. After we had worked together for a while, she told me that she liked me very much, but she wasn't sure that I could help her with her depressions, because I didn't make her angry enough. She also told me that there was a psychiatrist whom she had seen briefly who seemed to have the ability to truly anger her. But he was so good at it, she couldn't stay in the same room with him for any length of time. Perhaps, she thought, the best thing for her would be to see both of us at the same time.

I called her former analyst and told him about her suggestion. We met and decided that we could work together. So I saw her three times a week, including one session together with the other analyst. At first I couldn't imagine what my colleague was going to do. The patient had told me that he would have temper tantrums, but I couldn't believe that. (I later saw this analyst socially and was impressed with his kind nature.) This is an example of how he worked with her.

One day he came into the room where the patient and I were sitting. He was about ten minutes late and seemed very happy. The patient was sitting head down, looking very dejected. He said, "Hi, I had a wonderful dream last night and I'm hoping you're going to help me understand it."

There was no movement from the patient. Her head was still down.

He said, "Won't you help me with my dream?"

No response from the patient.

This time his voice was more insistent: "It's my dream, won't you help me?" Then he began pounding on a table. "I've been so good to you—I've helped you so much—and you won't even help me with one dream. What kind of a person are you?"

He went on and on, telling her she didn't care about anyone, and he was the most helpful person in the world. By now he was screaming, shouting, pounding, until finally I could see anger stir in the patient—in her body, in her face, in her eyes—and she said, "Okay, dammit, I'll help you."

We three had many such sessions. After about a year she told me that she had had enough help from my colleague, and suggested that from then on we continue with our individual sessions. Indeed, her mood was substantially improved and she was rarely depressed.

There was another young woman, mother of three small children, with a similar history of suicidal depression. After we had worked together for a while, to the point where she no longer seemed so depressed, her anger flared out unexpectedly. One day as I was in the middle of a session with another patient, she telephoned me, and said, "I have decided what I'm going to do. I am going to kill my children."

I heard her determined tone and knew this was a moment when I needed to call on everything I had in me. I said in a firm, unshaking voice, "You are to go to the nearest pet shop—there is one on West Tenth Street—and you are to buy the three biggest and fattest goldfish in the shop. You are then to go to the hardware store on Sixth Avenue between Tenth and Eleventh Street and you are to buy the sharpest scissors you can find, and then you are to go home and you are to cut the three goldfish into the tiniest possible pieces."

She said, "You are impossible!" and hung up, only to

call me back in a minute to say, "How can I cut up those poor goldfish?"

And of course my reply was, "How can you kill your poor children?"

They say the meek shall inherit the earth. But sometimes it seems as though the depressed mean to rule it—the way a sick person can sometimes tyrannize an entire household. In the case of depression, the disability is self-imposed, but it nonetheless serves as a license for persistent, provocative demands.

A young woman was becoming disenchanted with her very demanding man. She wanted to break off their relationship because his dark moods were too much for her. They argued about separating, until she was finally provoked into saying, "You must be off your rocker— you're always moping around, you always make as if you're the saddest person in the world."

"Yes," he said, "I am sick, and that's why you must love me and not leave me!"

6/
No more victims needed here

Recently, during one of our group therapy sessions, one of us joked, "We should have a sign made to put over our door: 'Through These Portals Pass Only Victims.' "

The other one quipped back, "I'd rather see it read: 'No More Victims Needed Here.' "

We are constantly astonished at the number of people who come to see us wearing the label "Victim."

They come crying, "Look at what's happening to me!" They profess themselves to be innocent of any responsibility for their situation. They are convinced they are incapable of doing anything to ease their plight.

The analyst cannot change the world for his patient. Working together, analyst and patient can hope to find a way of turning things around. Here the analyst often encounters the patient's need to be innocent. In order to preserve this sense of innocence, the patient insists on his impotence and thus forfeits any possibility of helping himself—as if to be able to help one's self is to admit blame.

I don't like to say so, but I've spent some time being sorry for myself and feeling like a victim.

If you can take responsibility for where your life is, if you can be "big enough" to say, "I've made a mistake, I've looked at things the wrong way. I wasn't all that smart," then possibilities open up and you put yourself in possession of the powers, of the strength, you previously denied you had.

Don't forget that if you were able to get yourself into trouble, you can get yourself out of it.

That all sounds very logical, but aren't there any real victims in this imperfect world?

Of course, but stay with us and try to keep an open mind. We are not saying that there isn't evil and injustice in the world, or that some people are not selfish and thoughtless and at times even cruel to each other. Life is often hard and unfair. But do you need to provoke additional hurts to *prove* how unfair the world is?

I don't know. I must confess I never looked at it that way.

A patient's recollection from childhood may help make this clearer:

"My brother was a few years older, and much bigger and stronger. I didn't have a chance in a fair fight with him. But I got to be pretty good at getting my licks in at strategic moments. I would time them for a moment when my father could come to the rescue quickly. Then I would give my brother a sharp and painful kick in the ankle. As he turned in pain and rage to clobber me, I would set up a plaintive howl and call to my father as witness and rescuer. Naturally, my father would administer summary justice to my brother, and don't you believe I didn't gloat."

He could remember giving the kick in the ankle in his childhood. In his adult life, he overlooked his own provocations and focused mainly on his detractors.

He doesn't sound like a very nice person.

Well, remember that he selected this way to defend or protect himself because when he was little he thought it was the only way possible. He gave himself no other choices. As we discovered later in his treatment, he was frightened of both his older brother and his father. The sad thing is that he carried them both with him into adulthood. He always had a certain look of wide-eyed innocence, he always hung on to his fear of men, and he always felt small. He was a convinced victim, and our job was to help him see how he was kicking the world in the ankle and not even knowing it. He was still the kid who was hitting and howling.

It sounds as if someone comes to you complaining about how the world is mistreating him, and you have to help him understand what he is up to.

Yes. Our task is to help people see how they arrange "happenings" in their own lives.

Here is another description from childhood:
"I must have been about seven. I found a book of matches. Knowing I was forbidden to light them, I went

into the bathroom and lit one after another, throwing each lit match into the toilet bowl. Then I touched a match to the sheet of toilet tissue that hung from the roll. To my horror, the entire roll began to smolder and the bathroom filled with smoke. I ran out in a panic and closed the bathroom door. So far, no one had seen me. But I knew there would be hell to pay, so I had to cover my tracks.

"I went into the kitchen, where my mother was cooking, and said, 'Ma, can I go to the bathroom?' She looked at me strangely and said, 'What's this?' I said, 'I have to go to the bathroom, is it all right if I go?'

"She said something about my talking nonsense, since I never needed permission before. Then she smelled the smoke. After she had put out the fire, which by now had charred the wall over the toilet tissue, she gave me a severe spanking.

"I felt outraged. Why should I be punished? It could have been done by any of my brothers or sisters. And besides, I thought she loved me best. Why should she jump to the conclusion that I had lit the fire? Hadn't I been asking for permission to go to the toilet? That should prove I hadn't been there. She was unfair!"

The same person had a similar experience during the same period of childhood. He attended a strict school where the pupils were struck over the knuckles with the teacher's ruler when they failed to memorize their daily text. For most of the year he had been teacher's favorite, but then he let up on his homework and began to do poorly. When he got his knuckles rapped, he became inwardly angry at the teacher. She became an enemy in his fantasies, unfair and cruel and to be defied.

These events are indicative of a thread that can be followed through the years. When he was an adolescent he provoked another incident where he felt victimized. He was the town high school football star, and captain of the team during an undefeated season. In the middle of an important game he had the option of accepting or declining a penalty for his team. Without looking to the coach for instructions, he replied testily to the referee's question as to the penalty option, "Well, what do you think we're going to take?"

He was sent off the field by the referee and reprimanded by the coach. This was the beginning of his feeling misunderstood and mistreated by officials and coaches. He sulked for weeks, lost his captaincy and didn't finish out the season.

He sure wasn't being his own best friend. But what was he getting out of it?

It can be a bit scary when you reach the top. The ambition to lord it over others could be showing. As mother's favorite, teacher's pet or team captain, there was the real and the fantasied envy of others—his father, brothers and other males. He was placating the men in his life: they no longer needed to feel envious. He was also proving his own strength, because he was able to provoke them and make them lose their tempers. As an adult, he continued to be unsuccessful so that he need not allow himself the full use of his fine mind and technical skill. He developed the provocative pattern of promising much and then disappointing. Eventually he would feel resentful of those who were not sufficiently understanding of his failures. He even became accident-prone.

To help him understand himself, I said, "In a choice between being the hammer or the anvil, you would rather be the anvil. The more hard knocks you take, the more noble you feel."

He said, "I guess that's very true. At least I know I'm

not the one who's hurting anybody. Besides, I've always been taught it is good to suffer. Didn't Christ suffer and die to make the world better for everyone? Don't people improve through pain and suffering?"

"Not necessarily," I said, "not through needless suffering. People tend to overlook Christ's plea to have the cup of suffering removed, if that be God's will. To hurt yourself needlessly or misuse your talents will never improve you or help anyone else."

This man's story is still unfolding. He seems to be going through a slow but steady awakening. He is allowing more of his real abilities to show and seems to be building toward a satisfying love life and career.

Is this another one of his big build-ups before the big letdown?

We have high hopes and good feelings, and the rest is up to him. At least he knows now that the choice is his.

Some people don't believe they have a choice. A very talented and successful dancer came to see one of us. In the course of one of our sessions, I asked, "How did you come to be a dancer?"

She replied resentfully, "Oh, it had nothing whatever to do with me. My mother's ambition was for me to be a famous dancer. She made me practice and dance every single day of my life."

Then I said, "You didn't have to do that. You must have wanted to."

"Not at all. I did not want to do it. How could I possibly have gotten out of it? I was only a little girl. She wanted me to be a dancer. She insisted."

I said, "I can think of two things off the top of my head.

One day when you were dancing, you could have fallen and broken your leg. Or you could have been a little clumsy. Who made you be so graceful? You wouldn't have become a famous dancer if you hadn't been so graceful."

What a wise thing you said to that woman.

Sometimes a patient is the wise one. A gifted lawyer had the irrational feeling that her mother was going to come after her with a knife. She had had this feeling for years, and could never understand it. During a session with her group, one of the men asked if anyone in the room ever had thoughts about parents making love. Several people in the group responded to his question, and the lawyer said, "Oh yes. I remember sleeping in the room next to my parents and hearing their sounds, and then feeling that my mother was going to come after me with a knife."

Another man interrupted, "Wait a minute. Wait a minute. Not so fast. You must have left a step out. You must have had a thought between hearing the sounds and feeling your mother was coming after you with a knife. Weren't you thinking something in between? Weren't you imagining yourself in your mother's place?"

She blanched, but as the color returned to her face, she said, "Now I know. Now I remember. I used to imagine myself in that bed in her place."

The punishment deserved a crime.

A woman came to see me, and when I asked, "Why are you here?" she said, "My husband is having an affair. The crazy thing is that I realized last week how I had arranged it all myself. That's when I called you. I want to know why

I did something so painful to me. I want to stop doing things like that.

"I remember meeting this girl, and thinking, John would love her, and thinking, How can I get them to meet? and thinking, He'll love her as much as I do, she's so pretty and talented and interesting.

"I arranged a meeting and I brought her home! Last week I discovered the two of them in bed, and I was outraged, until I realized it was all my fault."

She certainly knew she helped to victimize herself, but what about her husband's part in the affair?

Of course he has to answer for his own behavior, and even though the wife could see her own part in it, she was not about to take all the blame. But she knew he was always looking for affairs, and her friends would often ask her how she could stand having such a promiscuous husband. She thought she was only joking when she quipped, "If I weren't such a masochist, I would kill him."

I get the lady's humor and that connection between sadism and masochism. But how could she have gone on being a party to her husband's unfaithfulness?

In her life dream she was not worthy of having a man of her own. It always felt to her as if she were the one who was involved with another woman's husband. As she went along in her analysis, she learned how righteous it felt to be "the woman wronged," and not have to feel like the "wicked one."

So, strange as it may seem, she was more comfortable having another woman in the picture. It saved her from the pangs of guilt and anxiety. Her need to provoke the eternal triangle disappeared only when she could give up her fantasy of being the wicked temptress.

If you understand the crime of which you accuse yourself, you don't have to arrange a punishment and be the victim.

7/
The hole in the bottom of your sack

Aesop had a delightful way of describing people and their foibles. He told about the beggar's sack, two connected pouches, slung over the shoulder. One pouch was carried on the back and the other hung in front, on the chest. He said people put the faults of others in the pouch in front; their own faults they carried out of sight in the pouch behind.

What would be the modern version of the fable? Today we see ourselves carrying a saddlebag slung over a shoulder. In the pouch in front we carry the happiness, the satisfactions and gratifications of others; we carry our own out of sight, out of mind, in back.

That pouch in back has a hole in the bottom, so the things we might feel good about dribble out—our bag feels empty. No matter how much we try to put in, we feel deprived.

I've been listening carefully to your stories of people who are still living in the past, still living in their childhood, or who are living life dreams of anger and revenge, and those who are victims. Aren't all those people depriving themselves?

You're quite right. The truth is that everyone who is living a life dream contrived when he was young must be depriving himself of the fullness and richness of feeling truly alive in the present. These are people who are not only depriving themselves but who seem to have the additional goal of emphasizing their deprivation to themselves and to the world. They carry placards saying, "See, I have nothing."

I guess they are also trying to hide something.

Judge for yourself.

What would you think of a woman who came from modest beginnings, but whose husband succeeded well beyond what most people achieve, whose children are grown, who manages to have all the household help she can use, and who still has to find a way to make herself unhappy?

Her hobby is making pottery, but this woman can make exquisite self-torture out of what could be a satisfying and creative pursuit. She attends classes three afternoons a week, and she spends each morning of those days in agonized conflict over whether she can make herself go. She worries about whether her pots will collapse, whether the design will take and whether her classmates and teacher will like her work.

Of course, she does not keep these concerns to herself.

So her friends, her husband, her children, her sisters and brothers cannot say to her, "Isn't it wonderful that you have the leisure and freedom to pursue your interests? Isn't it great to have a husband who will deny you nothing, and is pleased to provide you with every comfort and convenience?" They certainly could not ask her, "How does it feel to be living so much better than everyone you grew up with?" They can only feel pity for this poor, tortured woman who has everything but can't enjoy it. This woman uses her feelings of deprivation to cover her guilt about the luxury of her life style.

Would you rather be pitied or envied?

An attractive model was in group analysis, primarily because of difficulties with her marriage. Her husband was moderately successful, but not quite successful enough to keep up with his wife's extravagance—particularly her insistence on taking taxis everywhere. The amount of time she spent actually modeling was very small compared to the time spent traveling to agents and auditions and on other errands—and, of course, she always went by taxi. She was not moved by her husband's protest about the extravagance, nor did she agree with his feeling that she devoted too much of her time to her mother.

One day she arrived for her session with her eyes red from crying as though in deep mourning. As the group rallied to comfort her, she sobbed out this story. On her way to the group, in a taxi as usual, she had started a conversation with the cabdriver. It turned out he had known her father and told her what a wonderful man he had been. A new person in the group thought from the way she carried on that her father had just died. But the others knew it had happened years ago, when she was twelve. They also knew about her taxi habit. What we had not known until this moment was that her father had been a cabdriver. She had been searching for her dead father, or at least for someone who knew him, all these years—and now she had found that someone.

With the help of her group the meaning of her behavior was uncovered. She had never felt right about leaving her widowed mother in order to marry; therefore, she neglected her husband for her mother and created dissension at home through her extravagance. The endless quest for father through interrogating the thousands of cabdrivers in New York was an unconscious way of dramatizing the message to mother: "Please don't be jealous. I don't have so much more than you. I am also deprived."

The group helped her to see that she was not responsible for her mother's state, that she did not help her mother by depriving herself.

Having less doesn't give another more.

Her father died when she was only twelve. Losing a parent when you are young is a real deprivation, isn't it?

It surely is, but why turn that feeling into a way of life?

One of the most touching stories in our experience is about a girl who had never seen her father, as her parents had separated before her birth. As a child she envied the other children who had daddies who came home at night and bought them presents and carried them on their shoulders. She took the few facts she could glean from her mother about her father and constructed an imaginary daddy who was tall and strong and handsome and went about the world making his fortune. He was a very important man, this daddy of her fantasies, who was very busy doing important things which demanded all his time and attention.

One day while she was sitting in my office—now a woman of twenty-five—I noticed something in the sweet childishness with which she sat perched on the edge of the chair, knees together, hands folded in her lap, that prompted me to say, "You look like a little girl waiting for her daddy."

Though it was not by conscious design, she had always remained that little girl whose daddy would come home any day—rich and famous, and bearing gifts. It was as though, in her appearance and her manner, she had been able to arrest the passage of time. As if to say, "How will my daddy recognize me if I'm not this little girl?"

She had kept herself from growing up and had deprived herself of her life. She went to work as though she were going off to school, and in everything else she did she acted like a sweet, charming little girl. She could allow herself to have what a child had, but she carefully avoided growing up. Her display of deprivation was for the benefit of the phantom daddy who might walk through the door at any moment. Then he could recognize her and know that she had been waiting loyally. My simple comment made it possible for her to begin to become aware of her self-deprivation and eventually to awaken from her dream.

Another young woman reminded us that it's very irritating to single people to have well-meaning friends and relatives pester them with the question, "Well, when are you going to get married?"

"I'm twenty-eight, and really quite content. I don't feel anything is missing in my life. I enjoy living alone, never feel lonely, have lots of friends, a good job, a lovely apartment, but it's beginning to get to me, the way everyone is hounding me about when I'm going to get married. Is there something wrong with me?"

The young woman who spoke those words in my office was convincing, and nothing that came out in the next few sessions served to belie her initial statement. She was an exception, she was not advertising her deprivation.

I was interested in what she did about her meals.

"You don't have to worry about me. I'm really into balanced menus. I eat properly—I'm very health-conscious. I feed myself very well. Each night that I'm home I cook a complete meal—soup or juice, meat, fish or chicken, fresh vegetables, salad and dessert."

I was amazed to hear this. Most other people of our acquaintance who live alone rarely cook dinner—unless they are having guests—and if they are spending an evening alone, settle for a piece of cheese or fruit, or open a box of cookies, or a can, or cook a TV dinner, or bring home a cooked hamburger, or eat leftovers. I was impressed with her concern for balanced nutrition, but it also became clear that something else was involved. She gave me some of her favorite recipes, and they called for pretty complicated preparation. I learned of her special fondness for fine china and linen, which she used even when she was dining alone.

After she had been in treatment for some time, it became clear to both of us that she was living in a dream. Her fantasy was that she was living with her daddy. She was the mommy and each night she cooked his dinner. Of course she couldn't have a life with anyone else, for that would mean a life without her daddy. Opening her eyes to the dream life of her existence was painful for her.

She no longer had the fantasy of the comforting presence of her father. Now for the first time she had to confront the loneliness of her life. But then she developed an interest in marriage, and eventually did get married. You can be sure her husband's first meals were not the usual unhappy experiments of so many new brides.

I can certainly see how that girl, through her deprivation, had achieved something she thought was pretty special. And she didn't even know that she was deprived.

On the other hand, we knew a man who pointedly deprived himself. I noticed that toward the end of each session he would start to get ready to leave even though we still had time left.

"What's your hurry?" I said one day. "What would happen if you just relaxed and sat there until the session came to an end?"

He said, "Why should you always tell me when it's over? Why should I hang around so *you* can kick me out? I'd rather go on my own time."

This exchange led us into a discussion from which it developed that the patient was always supercareful never to overstay his welcome anywhere. He was protecting himself against the unpleasant surprise of being told that his time was up. He also had a rather fully developed fantasy about how everything in life occurred in four-year cycles and he could muster some very convincing evidence on this point.

"Look," he said, "there is a new administration in Washington every four years, and in many other public offices. Four years and you're out! Then you're no longer such a big deal. You go to high school for four years, make the team, become a big shot in the senior class, and then you're a nothing when you get to college. The same story in college: You work your way up for four years—big man on campus finally, and then you graduate and again you're a nobody. You go to graduate school, and at first you have to ask your way to the men's room, then in four years you've got a title, but professionally you know you're only a beginner. That's the way life is."

There was a long pause, then he continued, "Have you ever noticed how a lot of marriages seem to go downhill after about four years?"

I said I hadn't.

"Well, mine seems to be going that way. We've been married four years, and it's getting dull, boring—nothing much to say to each other."

"I can understand that," I said. "You probably haven't got much to bring to your marriage, because you're sitting on the anxiety of waiting to be kicked out or graduated. Do you remember the first memory you told me last week?"

"Of course, I remember being sent to live with a strange family. My mother had gone to the hospital and there was no one else to take care of me."

"Why was she going to the hospital?" I asked.

"To have a baby."

"How much older are you than your younger sister?"

"Four years!"

That was it. That was the biggest shock of his young life—summary exile from the warmth and familiarity of the stable world he had always known, a world in which he was the only one, the crown prince, pampered and petted. It was never the same again, and he had made himself a most solemn, lifelong promise, as only a deeply hurt and deeply determined child can: it would never happen again. Never any awful surprises. He would know when his time was up. He would keep his eyes open. He would never be naïve and trusting and take anything for granted—never let down and never relax.

Because of his childhood pledge, he could not commit himself more than temporarily—to his marriage or to his vocation. To save himself that hurt of long ago, he denied himself.

I can see that he overdid it. But isn't there something to his point of view? Something bad can always happen. Isn't it smart to look ahead and protect yourself?

If you don't take a chance, if you don't have courage, you'll never have anything to protect. What our patient had to be helped to realize was that what had been such a crushing blow at four could never again be as devastating. He had more going for him. If something happened, it would still be a blow, but he would have himself to count on—it would not be as shattering. As a four-year-old, he still needed someone to take care of him; now he could take care of himself. It was only from the strong base of relying on himself that it was possible to really let go and get close to another human being. He deprived himself of this closeness and these feelings of love in order to make good that four-year-old's insurance policy.

It sounds as if he was afraid of something happening, but he didn't really know what he was afraid of.

That's what we mean when we emphasize the importance of facing your fears, facing your anxieties. In the course of growing up, we have all been told that it's not right to be afraid. So, very often you have to *know* that you are afraid before you can face your fear. Bravado isn't bravery.

It's good to keep in mind that you can be afraid, but that fear isn't all there is in you. It's a wonderful feeling to stop running, stand your ground and look your fear in the eye. You may discover that it's only a child-size fear, after all, and that you can handle it.

It's becoming clear to me that these life dreams help people control what happens to them. Since the script has been written beforehand, then the ending can't be much of a surprise.

Yes. You could call these life dreams an attempt to stay ahead of the game.

There was a young woman who cried a great deal during her sessions. She would come in, start to talk about something and then begin to cry, and hardly be able to continue speaking.

One day she came in and announced, "Tonight I'm going to tell my husband what he does that bothers me. I'm going to let him know how he mistreats me." And then she began to cry.

It did not seem to be the kind of weeping that makes you feel better, but rather the kind that just goes on and on. I said after a while, "For God's sake, you are not crying for now. You are crying for what you imagine is going to happen. You're going to tell him this, and he's going to leave you, and you will be abandoned. But it hasn't happened—it may never happen. Why cry now? You are writing out the script in advance."

She stopped crying, raised her head and said, "Why didn't you ever tell me this before?"

Actually, I'd been trying to tell her for some time, but she had not heard or I hadn't said it clearly enough so she could hear me through the crying. Now she understood. "That's right, I don't have to cry in advance. Maybe I don't have to cry at all."

Of course, she hadn't learned to cry in advance in my

office. She had done the same thing when she talked to her husband about anything important. Usually it exasperated him, and then she really had something to cry about.

Following this session she could talk to her husband without crying, so he could listen and they could have a more reasonable discussion.

You know, I have that kind of habit. I often like to look at the last chapter of a book before deciding to read it.

It's pretty harmless if you do it only with your reading and not with your whole life. But even with books, while you may avoid being disappointed, you can be depriving yourself of pleasant surprises as well.

I never thought of it that way.

Here's someone else who wrote the end of the story first.

There was a woman who returned to her therapy group after she had a baby. When the group asked how she felt, there was something very downbeat in her response. She murmured in a subdued voice, "I'm okay. Everything is nice, the baby is nice." (The word "nice" makes everything bland, colorless and without feeling.)

After she had gone on in this tone for a while, another young woman in the group could stand it no longer. "I have to tell you this. I'm very jealous. You have everything I want. You are beautiful, you have a husband who loves you, and now you even have a lovely new baby. I'm willing to change places with you."

The young mother broke out in smiles, and giggled. It was as if she could now openly admit to her joy. "You're right. I do feel that I have everything. I am happy, very happy. The baby is wonderful. I never knew my husband could be so gentle and caring and loving. I have everything I ever wanted." She had tried to anticipate and control how the group would react and had almost succeeded in doing herself out of legitimate satisfaction and pleasure.

It's worth paying attention when someone's mood doesn't match the occasion.

Many people seem to feel the amount of happiness in the world is limited; this young mother was living a fantasy in which her happiness would be resented because she believed it robbed others of their joy. She was protecting herself from the anger she anticipated. She underplayed her joy, to the point of feeling listless. When the other woman actually expressed her envy, it was a relief. The confrontation she had dreaded came to pass, and she could see its irrationality. She hadn't taken anything that didn't belong to her. Nothing she had done would prevent the other woman from having her own husband, her own baby. She did not have to deny and hide her real happiness. And the other woman, having expressed envy, was now free to be genuinely happy for the new mother.

So it's not just a question of what you have, but how you feel about what you have, isn't it?

That's true.

People have different ways of coping with feelings of being undeserving.

A successful businessman reported this striking incident:

"I was in the middle of a violent fight with my wife last night, when suddenly I felt calm inside, and I had this strange thought, 'Go ahead. Fight, fight—let's have a real mess here. Then tomorrow I'll be able to make a killing in the market!'" Here's the trade of love for money or power. He was willing to sacrifice his marriage to pay for business success.

We also had a patient who was a former champion

80

amateur boxer with over twenty consecutive knockouts to his credit. But in the style of the "counterpuncher," he could not deliver a blow with any kind of power behind it until he had first been hurt.

Success is often equated with that which is hostile and forbidden—like "killing" the opposition. Deprivation and suffering may be invoked to justify or atone for the audacity of succeeding.

Have you ever noticed the scrapping and arguing that often take place between brother and sister? Sometimes it seems this is the only way they can have contact with each other. Underneath there may be a great deal of love which can't be admitted. If brothers and sisters are lucky, when they grow up they can look back and see that it was all a cover-up for affection that was too embarrassing to admit.

We knew a married woman who not only failed to take that step, but even carried the same scrappy stance over into her marriage. Her husband was not a husband to her. He was her big brother. She was sure he considered her a pest and a nuisance, just as her brother had. She was always expecting to get into a fight with her mate, and of course she did.

We need hardly add that for reasons of his own, her husband played the part to which his wife had assigned him in her fantasy. However, he too was in therapy and began to change. He became more loving, less rejecting, less critical. Do you think this made the wife happier? Guess again. She went into a panic. It was as if her brother had betrayed the secret pact of their childhood. If she was not the pesty kid sister to her husband, then her inner world was awry. Her husband was ready to give her more, but she could only keep her balance by having less. Being the pest gave her a comfortable sense of identity—kept her world in place. To accept love from her husband, she had to give up the dream of her brother. Feeling deprived keeps someone with you.

For once, the parents aren't in the picture.

But everyone has them. Please understand we're not blaming parents. Rather, we are trying to show what can go on in the mind of a child as he tries to understand and control his destiny and the powerful figures of his childhood, and how this affects his life as an adult.

Growing up on a farm without central heating, as one of our patients did, is an experience most of us don't know much about. It was a poor place, and in the winter the farmer earned extra money by working at the mill in town. He left the house before daylight and drove through the snow to his job. When the engine of the father's car was coaxed into life, that was the signal for his young son to slip out of bed and climb in with his mother. What paradise! Here it was warm and cozy, and she smelled good and was so soft. His mother was tolerant of his snuggling-up and cuddling, even of his caresses and running his fingers through her hair. But if she became aware that he had an erection (yes, even four-year-olds), she would become very annoyed and summarily order him back to his own bed.

His problem when he came into therapy?
Impotence.

I know—don't tell me. Getting into bed with his wife must somehow have reminded him of those times with his mother when he was not allowed to have an erection.

More than just a passive reminder. Somewhere in his mind he was actively refusing to acknowledge the passage of time and the change in cast of characters. He could be free to be potent only if he gave up the early sensuous pleasures of sharing his mother's bed.

But it really sounds so wonderful.

It *was* wonderful, and no one can take that away. To give it up in the present doesn't mean he never had it in the past.

Children will bind themselves not only to a warm, soft mother but, paradoxically, also to a cold, hard, rejecting one.

The woman in my office was in a panic. She said, "I can't go back to him. Twelve years is enough. This is the end."

She was choking, gasping, as though she couldn't get enough air. I tried to calm her, but I didn't know her very well, since this was our first meeting. "You don't have to go back if you don't want to," I said.

"You don't understand. I can't. I can't go back."

Finally she was able to relax a bit and tell me something about herself and her early life. What stood out was the deprived relationship she had had with her mother. It was one of those situations in which the mother turns the tables and compels the daughter into the mothering role. The only crumb of appreciation the child got was from taking care of her mother. It seemed to me as I listened to her that she was keeping her mother with her, that she was continuing to deprive herself.

I tried to tell her that she really didn't want her husband to give her anything, to help her, because if he did, she couldn't continue to feel deprived. (She couldn't have the feeling of her mother with her.) Feeling deprived keeps someone with you.

Finally I said, "I know you are very upset and it is hard for you even to hear me. Can you hear me?"

"Yes."

"Well, will you humor me a little? *I* will be *you* and *you* be *your husband*."

She was confused, and I explained, "The reason I would like to do this is that I have never seen him. I want to know what he's like. Okay? Okay, now I'm you and I've just come home. What does he say?"

She as husband: "Hello. Let me tell you about my work today. It's very important. This big financing—"

Me as her (interrupting): "I can't listen to you today. I'm very upset. I need something."

She as husband: "Darling, I love you. Of course, anything you want."

Me as her: "Well, I feel just terrible, I can't even tell you what I need."

She as husband: "But I love you—whatever you want. I want to hear about you. I won't talk about my problems. What happened to you today? What did you find out about yourself?"

Then she stopped and said, "He isn't a monster. He's this wonderful man. He'll give me anything I want. I never asked him for anything. Of course he would give it to me. I can't wait now to go home and tell him."

About an hour later she telephoned me and said, "I am dancing and skipping through the streets of New York. I feel wonderful. I even feel like going to that party tonight—but I still look awful."

I said, "Go have your hair done and you'll look fine."

She said, "Are you still playing me?"

I said, "No, I'm myself now."

And then she said, "I feel so marvelous. But I feel a little sorry, it was all so simple."

I really hadn't understood that psychoanalysis can help so quickly. Everyone knows it takes years and years.

She did feel better after our first session—but that's not an analysis.

It took a series of sessions to help another man begin to understand the intricacies of his dream of deprivation. Some men who move from job to job manage to improve their position with each move. The man we are describing here would often change jobs, but to no apparent good purpose. Over a period of time we were able to discern a sequence that went something like this. He would go to work for a man with whom he seemed initially impressed. Gradually his enthusiasm would diminish. He would begin to find fault with the way his boss handled the work. Before too long he had himself convinced that he was by far the better man, much more worthy of being the boss. Once he got into this phase of resentment, feeling that his merit was unrecognized and that he was working for an incompetent, he had to look for another position. And the story would repeat itself.

Again he would find someone to put on a pedestal who could soon be proven not to belong there. He was reliving his favorite childhood game of playing daddy, a game which his mother seems to have encouraged. She would tell him how smart and strong he was and imply that his father did not amount to much in her eyes. This may have been fact or fantasy, but he certainly believed she preferred him to his father. Since his father was bigger and stronger, the son's superiority had to be kept a secret. To preserve this secret he had to throw his father off the track.

One day he was having a fistfight with another boy, just as his father was coming home from work. He immediately stopped fighting and pretended the other boy had hurt him. He rushed upstairs, crying to his mother that his father just stood there and watched him get beaten up. By this means he "convinced" his father that he was just a weakling and a crybaby, while "proving" to his mother that his father was no good. Privately he knew that he was smarter than either of them. And since he had deliberately stopped fighting, he could tell himself that he could have beaten the other boy if he had wanted to.

In his adult life he continued to play the role of the unsung hero, secretly better than anyone around. To play this game, he had to deprive himself of any opportunity to demonstrate what he could do with real responsibility.

He had started this game in childhood because in comparison to his father, he felt powerless. It was a kind of whistling in the dark—to give himself a spurious sense of strength. It never became real strength because he continued to be plagued with a gnawing sense of inadequacy reinforced by his mother's attitude toward men. After all, he was a man like his father. Every time his mother had put his father down, he could feel her hostility toward men. Every time he put his boss down, he was putting himself down as well.

This man deprived himself of his real abilities in order to retain the fantasy of his secret understanding with his mother. In the course of his analysis he was able to face the futility of continuing to feed this childhood dream. He began to feel better about himself, and to take genuine pride in his talents. As an added bonus, he discovered many things about his father which for the first time he could appreciate and admire. At the same time his friendships with men took on a new quality. He had always felt a bit uneasy with them, as though he was something of a fraud about to be discovered. Now he felt straightforward and genuine with other men, and it was a satisfying feeling. He had awakened to a fuller life.

I have heard of many dreamers and their dreams. Could I know some more about that moment of awakening?

We have a word-for-word transcript of a key session of analysis which shows how it happened for one particular young woman. Nothing has been left out except some irrelevancies and identifying information.

8/
Awaken
the
Dreamer

I'm so glad to be here. I've been feeling terrible, anxious, just awful . . . I feel better in here. This is a safe place for me.

I've been coming here for a couple of years, and I've learned a good deal. I know more about myself and my feelings, but here it is—I still feel awful sometimes. I even thought of killing myself again— Oh, don't worry—I won't.

I was thinking about a career, but it makes me feel anxious. Maybe that's why I've been feeling so terrible. What do you think?

Lucy, I listen to you, and what I hear is that I have to make you feel better.

I've been thinking about you and thinking that when I

see you I would ask you again: Where is *your will?* I don't have a sense of your being on your own side. I have to *want* for you. Where is your will?

Well, let me think about that—will. *Why, that's exactly right—you are right.*

What do you mean?

That makes me angry at myself—I haven't any will or will power except the will to destroy. If I really wanted to do something, I would do it.

You mean, you really believe that you'd be able to do something if you wanted to?

I really believe that. Now the problem is whether I really want to do it, or whether I use my will against myself to prove that I'm a loser—or just to exist without attracting attention.

Hardly. To be a loser in a family as successful as yours is certainly to attract attention.

We went out Sunday night with somebody who got into astrological signs—very heavily—and handwriting analysis, and gave a crit on Aries, which I am.

How did it make you feel?

I don't know. But he read through the signs of all our children, and they are very accurate—as general descriptions. Oh, and then he analyzed handwritings, and he looked at Steve's handwriting and he said, "You're kidding me—this isn't your handwriting. Write the way you really write," and Steve said, "That's really the way I write." He saw a lot of secrecy in Steve's handwriting.

Didn't you just love that?

I think it's accurate. I think he is very secretive.

What did he see in your handwriting?

I have a good handwriting. I have a very open, positive, intelligent, logical, artistic handwriting. I have a terrific handwriting. I'm very proud of it.

And you're modest, too!

And I'm modest.

You know, when you mentioned will, I felt better about being here. I felt more positive . . . about a purpose that I could really work on. Will—I could make anything happen for myself that I wanted to, really wanted to.

This week was kind of dead. We made love on the weekend, and we haven't had sex very much at all and both of us are sort of relieved, and I was very angry and told him that we're childish in bed.

He got very angry and said he had told me that when he got home from group last week, and I said, "No, you didn't. I would know that," and he said, "No, I told you—now you're using that against me." And he said that one of the things he had discussed in his analysis was that we have to stop treating each other as children, but he hadn't said in bed, he hadn't said sexually. And maybe that stuck in my mind. But then, what did stick in my mind was that I didn't have to be a victim of someone else's behavior, and it became very clear that whatever my sexual problems are, there are two of us in bed—and we haven't had sex since and I'm not particularly happy or sad.

For the first time in our marriage we left it that sex was a two-way proposition—that it wasn't just my fault.

That would help you to feel better.

I feel better, but I still would like to have some good sex because I feel sexual. I don't really know what he discusses in his analysis. He's very secretive—and I don't want to spend this session on him. But because I feel more in charge of myself, I have a clearer view of him.

I'd love to have a clearer view of *you.*

Me? Me, I'm lazy and I'm terrified. I'm not really lazy, I'm scared. I'm scared of sticking my neck out and getting my head cut off. I'm scared because I don't have my will.

Who does?

I have given my will to my father!

Can you tell me something about that?

No. I could just see this very big father . . . It's a way of giving myself. It's a way of giving myself sexually, I gave him my only . . . that which makes me go . . . my will. I gave it to him.

A hell of a way to live your life.

Yeh, because . . .

Do you feel what you're saying—because I can almost touch it.

Well, I could feel it. I can see I gave him my life—I just gave it over to him.

Okay. So do you want it back?

I don't know. (I just know that I am not in possession of my will.)

Right.

It's like there's a car and it has my life in it. And what I do is I run alongside of it and I'm very, very tired all the time from keeping up. But I'm really not in charge of which way that car is going to go—whether it's going to turn left or right—but I've just got to keep up with it and keep up with it, and whichever way it goes, I have to go along with it.

What happens if you get in the car?

First of all I'd stop and rest.

When you get in?

Right.

And then what? Who is driving the car?

My mother.

Your mother is driving the car?

My mother is driving the car—I have to get into the driver's seat.

How will you get into the driver's seat?

I'm going to have to push her out of the car. I feel that's very rude.

Where will she go?

She'll have to run alongside the car—is the way I see it.

Can you do that to a poor old lady?

No! How can I do that to my mother—make her run as hard as I ran and get her so tired.

So what you're saying is—"It's a choice."

It's her or me. If I could really believe that. But I do really believe that—because I'm not making it up.

You really had the image of your mother in that car?

Yes—I guess, too, because Nancy was in the car with me today and she wants to have my driver's license. It's a repeat. I remember as a little girl—just yearning to drive a car, and riding alongside my mother and pretending and pretending.

Yes. And if she has your license, it would be as if you had your mother's license.

Right. As if she had my mother's car . . . my mother's man . . .

As if there's only one woman and one man in the whole world!

Well now, if I got in the car and I was driving, I could drop my mother off in an old-age home.

You said Nancy wanted your driver's license—your car. The question is: Are you running alongside your mother's car, or was it your car? You're big enough to have your own car—you're not Nancy—you're not three years old. Why are you still running after her car?

Nancy's or my mother's?

Your mother's. Everyone has a car except you. I could understand your running after her car when you were Nancy's age—when you were a little girl—but you are not three years old any more. You're old enough to have your own car.

You're right. The question is: Why aren't I driving my own car, and she drives her car . . . ?

She doesn't have to go to an old-age home. She doesn't have to be out in the cold. She doesn't have to be running after you. In your head, there's only one car.

I understand that. The question I want to answer is: If I got in my own car, where would I go?

Okay, that's the question I want you to answer. Where would you go?

That's funny. When I had my orgasm, it was like racing along a road. Oh—I don't know where I'd go. So many things have happened this week that are all like signs. If I don't take care of myself, it's going to go past me.

Wait a minute. Are you giving up the image of where you go? Try.

No, I'm trying to get the image together. I would go . . . where I was happy.

You had such a wonderful image—of yourself in a car and your mother driving her car. Where would you go?

Okay—I'd go to McDonald's.

You'd go to McDonald's!

I'll tell you something else about cars, and the lady on the block who killed her children. She took her children into the car, and she put on the gas and they all died of carbon monoxide poisoning in the garage. And when your mother takes you into the car, she takes you to all the places you don't want to go—drags you through snowstorms, up hills. The car gets stuck, she gets out, she shovels the snow, she puts cinders in the road—she has cinders in the trunk so she can make the hill to go to grandma's.

But you don't have to go to all these places—if you get into your own car.

Where do I want to go? Well, I don't want to go to the garage with that lady. I want to go home. I want to go into my mind.

Which is home?

In my head.

Try to keep going—keep moving.

I see a comfortable room. I don't know whose room. It seems where I want to go is . . . I want to go back to when I was little, to the little house.

But this is your own car. You can go any place. Next thing you know, you'll be visiting your sick, crippled grandmother.

Ugh—no. Maybe there was a point where I switched it off when I was little. I changed directions. I've always felt there was some point that was very important to me—where I sold myself out—almost a date. And I always had a feeling that I would have to go back to that, to go ahead. Now I don't know whether that is tricking myself. What do you think?

I'm still thinking of where you're going with your car. It's your choice. It's not your mother dragging you with her—against your will.

Well, obviously it hasn't been against my will all these years, because I'm the one who's running alongside her car, because I want to go where she's going to take me. So it hasn't been against my will all these years. It's been exactly what I wanted.

So if you got into your own car, you'd still be running after her.

No, I didn't say that. I don't think I would go anywhere. I don't want to go anywhere, I'm tired of going.

Yes, you could stop running.

I could just stop. Right.

But you can't do that if you don't have your own car.

I don't even need a car. I could just stop—period—and let it happen. If I'm always worried about which way that car is going to go and running alongside of it, and we got off track when I said I wanted to get in . . . I don't want to get in, I just want to stop running beside it.

Okay, so why can't you?

I could. But then I'd feel all alone. <u>You know, I'd feel without purpose</u>. I've spent so many years running, that it's a new feeling . . . I know what I'm talking about. There's a time when you realize you're just . . . "self." That's it.

    There is no more, you're not tied to them, not tied to the past. You're just there. There is a continuity, but you're not tied to it. It's just a continuity. It's like a thread that unwinds. It's behind you.

Okay, it's your will to run alongside that car.

It has been my will to run alongside that car.

What's the thing that made you run?

I want her to love me. I want to go with her.

If you had to pick a time when it started . . . ? It doesn't matter if it's right.

I don't know. Maybe she threatened to leave me at home and screamed and yelled at me and I was afraid to stay home, and I begged her to take me along even though I hated where she was going. It was better to be with her—even though I didn't want to be where she was going—than to be alone in the house. She never left me alone, except to run into stores.

You said—if you got out of the car, you would be very lonely. Do you still feel you would feel lonely?

Well, I felt it when I said it—yeah.

You can't count on yourself?

No, I can't. That's where my will comes in. I can't count on myself to give myself any support.

Why not?

I can't. I can just count on myself to kick myself.

But what happens when you count on yourself? Isn't that the same as kicking your mother out of the car?

Well, obviously, it's not really. Because if I count on myself, then it just means she goes on her way and I go on my way, and I haven't kicked her out of the car—I don't want to get in the car. She'll stay there. She'll go where she has to go.

Is it that you'll feel lonely because you don't know what's happened to her?

No, that's not the question at all. I don't know what will happen to me. I'll have to give up what I know day in and day out—what I can count on.

What a thing to count on.

Well, in my case, all it's resulted in—in behavior—is constantly having to tear after something—groceries, or whatever. Whatever . . . just always working . . .working . . .

When you do that, you're with her.

I'm with her. I'm running after her. She doesn't even want to hold me. That's it. She has already given me up.

So the truth is—you really are counting on yourself.

Yes. Of course. I made a decision and I'm running after her.

Not only that. You do have to do everything yourself—because she's really out of reach.

That's right.

So it's all an illusion about being with her.

Right. Which is very lonely too, which also keeps me in a state of abandonment.

But you know that when you were little and you ran after her, you really needed her, to protect you.

Yes, and it would be her style—as it has been my style—to deny that, when she was out of sorts with herself.

You do have yourself. Lots of people count on you. Steve counts on you. The children count on you. What happens if you count on yourself? What happens if you wake up from the dream of running after her?

Well . . .

What did you just think, because my ears popped.

Oh, they did?

I know you didn't say anything. But what was . . . ?

Oh, I woke up a woman. That's what I thought . . . like a long sleep. And, well, Prince Charming is the thing that was going through my head.

And we know who Prince Charming is . . .

My father.

Not so very charming.

You've never met him. Give him a chance.

You mean all that stuff you've been feeding me all along isn't true? Now he's charming?

He is such a multifaceted person. Well, obviously no, I have to wake up by myself—I can't count on him. In other words, I'm running myself into a crazy state of exhaustion, figuring when I drop he'll pick me up. That's also in it?

It's hard to give it up—right?

I've got the whole thing worked out.

It's so neat.

I run and run and run, and when I drop he'll pick me up. That's what makes Sammy run. That, in the end, his mother will take care of him.

It is an awful lot to give up.

Well, it's been keeping me going for a long time, and now if I give it up, I don't know really what's going to replace it—except for me—and I don't know really if I've got their craziness that I've been living with all these years. I don't really know what mine is going to be.

It can't be any worse.

Just different, and different is different.

I have such a sense of you as a whole person. It feels good. Sometimes you come in here and you are like that— whole.

I'm more and more whole. Except with me, I'm such a late starter.

Who stops you from being this woman.

I stop myself.

Do you think I'd like you to be a whole person?

I know you would—yes. I think you would. I've separated you from my mother in many ways. It doesn't mean I feel any affection for you, because I have a lot of trouble feeling affection for anybody.

You hardly ever feel affection for yourself.

I try.

It's really good liking you, it really is—it feels good. But let's get back to your mother. If you always go with your mother, then you will never catch her.

That's right. She'll drive off into the sunset and she'll go to my father. Then I'll have to stop picking on them. I'll have to give them up—together—if I let go of her. So in running after her, I'm really keeping track of what she's doing with him. It's very clear to me. It means I have to let her have him.

So many things happened to me this week that are kind of weird. It must be because I'm giving out signs that I want to do something. But I can't do anything. A girl I know called me up and said, "Let's have lunch." She'd like to write a children's book and she wants me to do the illustrations. Her son and my son play together. So many mothers seem to be doing things. I never noticed before. I should be doing something. I should work, or something. If I could stop running after the car, I could do something. I think I would really like to do something on my own, maybe the illustrations for this book—or who knows? I don't want to go to work for someone. I'm not sure, maybe that would be the same thing as running after the car. I haven't stopped to take a look and see what I could do. Does that make sense to you?

It could—it sounds good. I mean, you could use it for yourself or against yourself.

But I would like to try to do the illustrations for that book.

But what importance would your life have, if you weren't running after the car? It's such a dedicated life.

I wouldn't be anybody. I want to be somebody. This way, at least I'm a roadrunner. I really want to be somebody. That's why I couldn't write the book myself—nobody in my writing has a will, everybody is a victim. It's very boring writing—it's not fun to write and it's not fun to read. If there's nobody who has a will, there is no hero.

It takes a great deal of will to run after that car for so many years.

Yeah, but what a fool! Who is interested in that fool?

Of course, if you only see yourself as a fool, then you don't see what you get from running after that car.

It seems stupid. I don't see me as a fool—I think I'm a smart person to come to that image. I think I'm a smart person to sit here and be able to realize today that really what I've been doing is chasing her, and I'm chasing her to make sure that she isn't with my father. I'm keeping tabs on her. As long as I'm after her, then I know where she is.

Yeah—you can't take your attention off that.

Right. I'm fixating on it and it keeps me busy all my life, and I'm a smart person to realize that . . . but I don't know what I could do with my smartness for myself.

You have to know what you get from running after that car before you can stop running.

I have a feeling that I get an attachment—that it's what keeps my heart beating.

All right—but also, that it takes a lot of will.

To stay alive, it takes a lot of will—that's what I hear you saying.

To run after that car takes a lot of will.

That's keeping me alive. I think that in my fantasy—if I stop, I die. It's just that simple. So I'm really just running and running and running, and I'm not alive and I'm not dead—but it's better than being dead.

Who'd get you?

I just would lose my identity. I would just be a speck.

I believe that. But I believe that underneath, you believe there is someone who is going to get you.

I don't feel threatened.

As you are running after that car, your mother can keep an eye on you, too.

I was just going to say that all the people who are

watching me would kill me, but I don't believe they would kill me. They would just watch me, and then would laugh, and they would say finally she stopped—ha-ha-ha.

That's death—to be made such fun of.

Right. They would laugh at me. I'm running from their laughter. Well, I see my grandmother and grandfather in there and a lot of cruel people. There were lots of cruel people in my childhood. They were cruel to me as a child because they gave no credit for humanity to a child. A child wasn't a human being. It was not a human being to be a child. I had a very clear feeling of that. The child was a problem. The child got sick. There was no humanity. Running makes me feel alive, and running makes me feel human, and running after her to someplace where I can get away from their looking and laughing. Also—that she'll take me someplace that will belong to me as a child.

How will your mother feel if you stop running?

Well, you see, in my fantasy I must believe that I'm going to take her to the place where she can be a mother and I can be a child, which is exactly why I went and had four children in six years, and when I really was doing something that I liked—you know, working as a cartoonist for that man. But I really wasn't . . . what the hell, I really couldn't, because my mind was dead. I mean, I was running there too, I was a perfect "go-for" person. So that's not true to say that if I had stayed and worked, I would be where she was, because she obviously has a good mind. She is in charge of her mind. I mean that other woman—the mother I had lunch with, which just made me feel . . . overwhelmed. Steve said, "How did it make you feel?" and I said, "It made me feel very unhappy." But not defeated.

Any time you want to—

I could turn my mind on.

And more.

But let's go back to where we were. If I stopped running, then my mother would go to where she is going to be a good mother and I won't get there and nobody will ever love me.

So you won't be able to change your childhood. You're running so that you can change your childhood.

That's exactly right. I'm running to go to the meadow in my mind—where there is one tree and there's a grassy knoll and the sun is shining and the sky is blue and we have a picnic and where I feel calm inside and not always winded and frightened. Which is exactly the way my mother talked about her own childhood too—the terror . . . just terrified. And she gave . . . me . . . that was her gift to me.

So your life is devoted to redoing your life.

Right. So I'm always running, running, running, running, running—and I never get past the present point, which is the past.

So the truth is, if you give up running, you won't be able to change your life back there, and if you don't give up running, you won't be able to change it either.

If I give up, I won't be able to change my life.

And if you don't give up, you still won't be able to change what happened to you when you were a child.

Right. That's why I'm so worried about getting older—

and I am—and so worried about finding that I'm in my thirties and it came so quickly.

Because you're still back there.

Yeah. It's not supposed to be now—it is supposed to be then. Maybe now after today now *will be* now.

Lucy, maybe now you will be able to use your will for each day, for the present, and you won't feel so compelled to run after her.

It wouldn't be possible for me to feel the same after today.

It was true—after that day Lucy's life was never the same.

She was no longer preoccupied with her parents and she had more to give to herself, her husband, her children. Since she was more open with her husband, she discovered him to be less secretive with her.

She began to awaken to a life with hope, trust, affection, love, vital energy and a will of her own.

9/
Now is now and then is then

Every life needs a direction, a purpose. Without goals, we drift uncomfortably. So at every stage in life we must face making sense out of existence by making decisions about

what is more important,
what is less important,
what is safe,
what is frightening,
what is satisfying,
what is empty.

The judgments made in childhood must be reviewed and revised with the passing of the years. What was important to a child cannot be equally important to an adult. If the perceptions and judgments of childhood are not consciously updated, one finds oneself "grown" but not "grown-up," and keeping alive the distortions of the past.

It is not easy to let go the outworn life dreams of childhood. Courage and uncompromising honesty with oneself make possible the moment of awakening. It is necessary to be aware of and to fight the recurring temptation to go back to the familiar notions of the past. The resolve to see this past through is strengthened by remembering that a new, adult view of life can be more in touch with the present. It is only by seeing the present clearly that it is possible to cope with the world as it is, let alone build a better one.

When one's energies can be concentrated on the *now*, not the *then*, one can truly be

Awake and Alive.

About the Authors

MILDRED NEWMAN, M.A., and BERNARD BERKOWITZ, Ph.D.,
are married to each other. They are psychoanalysts and
psychologists, and practice in New York City.

Ville de Montréal

Feuillet de circulation

À rendre le

	0 3 AOU '92	
1 8 FEV 1990	27 AOU '92	
2 8 MAR 1990	0 5 DEC '92	
	0 4 FEV '93	
0 2 JUIN 1990	24 MAR 01	
0 2 OCT 1990	Jan 5	1037
2 9 JAN 1991		
1 0 FEV 1991		
28 SEP '91		
17 Oct '91		
1 8 NOV '91		
2 3 FEV '92		
0 5 MAR '92		
1 2 AVR '92		

06.03.375-8 (03-83)